AUTUMN COLORS *of* KYOTO

PHOTOGRAPHS BY   Hidehiko Mizuno

Kayu Mizuno

Yasutaka Ogawa

KODANSHA INTERNATIONAL
Tokyo • New York • London

AUTUMN COLORS *of* KYOTO

A Seasonal Portfolio

PAGE 1: An antique lacquer bowl with a Japanese maple motif.

PAGES 2–3: Autumn foliage against the main gate of Nanzen-ji temple.

PAGES 4–5: An autumn view from the precincts of Yoshiminedera temple.

Distributed in the United States by Kodansha America LLC, and in the United Kingdom and continental Europe by Kodansha Europe Ltd.

Published by Kodansha International Ltd., 17–14 Otowa 1-chome, Bunkyo-ku, Tokyo 112–8652.

Photographs © 2008 Hidehiko Mizuno, Kayu Mizuno, and Yasutaka Ogawa. All rights reserved. Printed in Japan.
ISBN 978-4-7700-3093-1

First edition, 2008
17 16 15 14 13 12 11 10 09 08   10 9 8 7 6 5 4 3 2 1

   Library of Congress Cataloging-in-Publication Data

Mizuno, Hidehiko, 1968-
  Autumn colors of Kyoto / photographs by Hidehiko Mizuno, Kayu Mizuno, Yasutaka Ogawa.
    p. cm.
  ISBN 978-4-7700-3093-1
  1. Kyoto (Japan)--Pictorial works. I. Mizuno, Kayu, 1969- II. Ogawa, Yasutaka, 1975- III. Title.
  DS897.K843M59 2008
  915.2'186400222--dc22

                         2008032471

www.kodansha-intl.com

CONTENTS

F O R E W O R D

Mention autumn colors and inevitably the riotous foliage of maples springs to mind, their radiant leaves being for many the epitome of that season. But in the world of Japanese garden design, maples can never take center stage. Since early times in the Japanese garden the leading role has been enjoyed by the evergreens, such as pine and *maki* (*Podocarpus macrophylla*) that retain their foliage all year round. Maples, which lose their leaves with the arrival of winter, are invariably relegated to a supporting role.

It is nevertheless true, however, that the maple has been much loved by the Japanese for centuries, and even today people happily travel long distances to savor the spectacle of autumn maples in the country's most famous gardens. Why is this?

Transforming in late autumn from green to yellow, then yellow to red, maples burn bright in a momentary blaze of glory, taking the edge off the stark rawness of evergreens, and awakening seasonality in the whole of the garden in a fiery explosion of color. Then, having played this pivotal role masterfully, they shed their leaves without remorse.

In this process of transformation, maples remind us of the final blaze of glory in our own lives. In their brilliance there is transience, in their joy there is sorrow—for centuries they have provided powerful inspiration to countless people. Maples resonate with Japanese sentiments of life and death and aesthetic sensibilities that attach great importance to purity, and the beauty and grace with which leaves, flowers, and people, take their leave of this world.

With the relentless march of civilization, we have all but forgotten what it means to "wait for the seasons." Gazing at the bare trees of winter and envisaging them bursting into bud in spring; seeing them covered in the lush foliage of summer and conjuring up images of chilly autumn winds—today we seem to be losing these imaginative powers so adored by our forebears. But still those powers live on somewhere in our hearts, which is why on a chance day in autumn, an unforeseen glimpse of a single leaf can move us so much.

The secret of Kyoto's breathtaking autumn hues lies in the airy lightness of the abundant, delicate leaves, with their sharp contours and almost translucent redness, that adorn the landscape. With each individual tree displaying a vibrant gradation from green through to scarlet, there is plenty to delight the viewer. Furthermore, the trees change color in turn across the whole of Kyoto, starting with the city and moving to the hills, creating an indelible autumn landscape of kaleidoscopic charm.

Autumn colors dazzle for the moment between departing autumn and oncoming winter. Make sure you take the opportunity to witness their breathtaking beauty, a beauty that could only be created by nature.

Jihei Ogawa XI

Grandmaster of Ueji Landscape Design House

◀ Detail from a 16th-century painted screen titled *Kanpuzu Byobu* by Kano Hideyori. Designated as a National Treasure.

HOW TO USE THIS BOOK

■ This book divides Kyoto into its five traditional areas: Rakuchu (Central), Rakuto (East), Rakusai (West), Rakunan (South) and Rakuhoku (North), and lists the best-known sites for autumn colors in each.

■ The numbers in the text correlate to those on the map pages at the back.

■ The map pages also provide an address and contact details for each listing.

■ For reference, the following are the periods of Japanese history relevant to the places in this book:

PERIOD NAME	APPROXIMATE DATES
Heian	794–1192
Kamakura	1192–1333
Muromachi	1336–1573
Azuchi-Momoyama	1573–1603
Edo	1603–1868
Meiji	1868–1912

RAKUCHU

Central Area

洛中

Detail from a Noh costume with
Kyoto-style embroidery.

1 京都御所 Kyoto Imperial Palace

Behind this Gishumon Gate in the heart of Kyoto lies the palace, just north of the center of Kyoto Imperial Park. Its extensive grounds, enclosed by roofed earthern walls, contain many buildings of great historical significance, including the Shishinden, which was used for official ceremonies and government business, and the Seiryoden, the emperor's personal quarters. The present building was constructed in 1855, and is a fine example of early architectural styles. Permission must be obtained from the Imperial Household Agency before visiting.

2　廬山寺

Rozan-ji Temple

Initially constructed in Funaoka-yama in the mid-Heian period, Rozan-ji was moved to its present location in 1573. The *hondo* (main hall) and other principal buildings were transferred from the Sento Imperial Palace and rebuilt here in the 19th century by order of Emperor Kokaku. The "Genji Garden" in front of the *hondo*, formerly the site of the residence of Murasaki Shikibu, author of *The Tale of Genji*, is composed of moss and white gravel, with bellflowers adding to the vista in summer. The *Oni no Horaku* ceremony, featuring dancing demons and held at the *Setsubun* festival in February, is also worth a look.

3 Shimogamo Shrine

下鴨神社

Shimogamo Shrine, which along with Kamigamo Shrine is famous for May's *Aoi Matsuri* festival, is reputedly the oldest shrine in Kyoto. Venerated by the Heian Court, it appears frequently in the literature of medieval Japan. Shown here is the *Tadasu no Mori* ("Forest of Truth") that extends across the southern grounds. It is an expanse of ancient forest, home to many large trees. The main hall, thatched with cypress bark, is a National Treasure, and is located at the end of the shrine's tree-lined approach. The hall is an 1863 reconstruction, but its elegant lines retain echoes of Heian times. Shimogamo Shrine is a designated UNESCO World Heritage Site.

4 Myoken-ji Temple

妙顕寺

Myoken-ji dates back to 1321 and the founding of Nichiren Shonin's first Kyoto prayer hall. It flourished as the headquarters of the Nichiren Sect, but was moved several times due to a succession of calamities. Destroyed in the Great Tenmei Fire, a deadly conflagration that struck Kyoto in 1788, Myoken-ji, including the main hall seen here, was rebuilt in its present form in 1834. The temple is also the gravesite of the famed Edo-period artist Ogata Korin.

A carved silver and red copper *koro* incense burner created by contemporary Kyoto craftsman Yoshinaga Nakamura. The extremely delicate work required two years to complete.

5 梨木神社 Nashinoki Shrine

Built in 1885, tranquil Nashinoki Shrine rests in a small enclave of trees, and is dedicated to Sanjo Sanetsumu, who was a key figure in the Meiji Restoration of 1868, and his son Sanetomi. Nashinoki Shrine is also renowned for its *hagi* (bush clover) that blooms in riotous profusion in autumn.

6 立本寺 Ryuhon-ji Temple

Ryuhon-ji, said to date back to the 14th century, is famous for its hall dedicated to Kishimojin, the goddess of safe childbirth and child rearing. A series of fires led to several relocations throughout the medieval period, and the temple found its present site around the middle of the Edo period. The extensive grounds, which include four sub-temples, are a riot of cherry blossom in spring and lotus flowers in summer.

7 清浄華院 Shojoke-in Temple

Shojoke-in was founded in 860 by Imperial Decree as a prayer hall in the grounds of the emperor's palace. Subsequently relocated, it arrived at its present site in 1585. Over the centuries the temple was ravaged by a series of fires, and the current complex is a Meiji-period reconstruction. Its origins closely tie it with the Imperial Family, and it contains many royal graves.

[8] Myokaku-ji Temple

妙覚寺

This view is from the main hall of Myokaku-ji in Nishijin, which was founded in 1378, and moved to its present location in the 16th century following fire and reconstruction. Every building in the complex, including the main hall, is worth a visit, while the cemetery contains the graves of Kano Eitoku and other members of the Kano family, who dominated Japanese painting for generations. The temple is especially famous for its spring cherry blossoms and dramatic autumn tints.

RAKUTO

Eastern Area

洛東

Folding fans in the Kyoto style.

Tofuku-ji Temple

Autumn transforms the valley view of Tofuku-ji Temple's Tsuten Bridge into a kaleidoscope of colors, seen here and on the next spread. Starting in 1236, Tofuku-ji took nineteen years to complete and became Kyoto's largest temple complex. The principal image enshrined here is the Shaka-nyorai (also known as Shakyamuni, the embodiment of virtue). The main gate is a designated National Treasure, along with the meditation hall, baths, and latrines. All are Momoyama-period originals and priceless Zen architectural legacies. The *hojo* (abbot's quarters) garden, noted for its distinctive checkerboard pattern, dates from 1938.

10 清水寺 Kiyomizudera Temple

One of Kyoto's best-known temples, Kiyomizudera, believed to have been constructed in the 8th century, has long been venerated among ordinary people as the center of medieval Kannon (the bodhisattva of compassion) worship. The main hall, with its famous balcony extending far out from the hillside, is of unconventional construction and is a designated National Treasure. The principal image, an eleven-faced, thousand-armed Kannon, is concealed from view and only uncovered every thirty-three years, although a replica is on display at other times. The grounds stretch across the base of Mt. Otowa, and are a riot of cherry blossoms in spring, and fiery reds in autumn. The temple is a designated UNESCO World Heritage Site.

An antique *unkinbachi* bowl with a maple leaf and cherry blossom motif. This is the work of Nin'ami Dohachi (1783–1855), a celebrated *kyoyaki* (Kyoto ware) potter of the late Edo period.

Nanzen-ji Temple

The Zen temple Nanzen-ji, founded in 1291, is one of Kyoto's largest temples. This giant *sanmon* (main gate), an iconic image of the Nanzen-ji, is a 1628 reconstruction, and offers panoramic city views from the top. The *hojo*, which is a designated National Treasure, contains Kano-school painted sliding doors, and the hojo garden is a renowned example of the *karesansui* (dry landscape) type. Intersecting the temple's extensive grounds is an aqueduct that in Meiji times formed part of the Lake Biwa canal, a legacy of Kyoto's modernization.

12 金戒光明寺 Konkai Komyo-ji Temple

Konkai Komyo-ji, a major Jodo Shu (Pure Land Sect) temple of similar status to Chion-in (another Jodo temple in Kyoto), is said to have its origins in a prayer hall established by Jodo Shu's founder Honen Shonin (1133–1212) in 1175. Up the stone steps from the massive entrance gate, buildings—including the hondo, Amitabha hall (Amitabha is the principal Buddha of Jodo Shu), and the three-tiered pagoda seen here—sit in stately dignity on expansive grounds. Legend has it the Amitabha hall was rebuilt in 1605 from the same timber as that used for the Daibutsu hall of Hoko-ji Temple in Kyoto.

13 | Konpuku-ji Temple

金福寺

Konpuku-ji, founded in 864, has been called the spiritual home of haiku. On the grounds of the temple is a hermit's retreat where the priest Tesshu welcomed and forged a close friendship with the much revered "Saint of Haiku" Matsuo Basho (1644–94). The retreat, seen above, was subsequently named the Basho-an. After Tesshu's death the retreat fell into ruin, but was rebuilt in its present elegant incarnation by the poet Yosa Buson (1716–84). Best visited in late autumn for its fiery tints and sasanqua camellias.

14 | 哲学の道 | Path of Philosophy

This path, running along the Lake Biwa canal from Ginkaku-ji Temple to Nyakuo-ji Shrine, was a favored route of the philosopher Nishida Kitaro (1870–1945) on his contemplative strolls. Along the way are temples such as Ginkaku-ji and Honen-in, plus an array of shops and cafes, making this a popular walk. Furthermore, with cherry blossoms in spring, fireflies in summer, and a spectrum of changing colors in autumn, pleasant views are assured here any time of year.

15 青蓮院 Shoren-in Temple

Shoren-in began as priests' lodgings on Mt. Hiei, later becoming a *monzeki-jiin* (a temple whose head priest is an imperial prince) when a son of Emperor Toba built a palace there. This *shinden* hall is a former palace of the Empress Tofuku Mon'in that was later moved to the site. The Kachoden (guesthouse) offers views of the main garden, and is said to be the work of legendary landscaper Soami, while the Garden of Kirishima is credited to be the work of Kobori Enshu. Illuminations add to the temple's allure in spring and autumn.

Anraku-ji Temple

Anraku-ji, a vision of autumnal beauty with its leaf-sprinkled, thatched *sanmon* gate seen here, was originally a prayer hall of Honen Shonin. In the 13th century, two ladies from the court of retired Emperor Gotoba received enlightenment here and secretly absconded from the court, incurring the wrath of Gotoba, who ordered the banishment of Honen and the death of two of his monk disciples. A tower dedicated to the souls of the two monks was later built, and became Anraku-ji. Statues of the individuals involved in the incident can be found in the temple's hall, monuments to their tragic story.

Antique gold lacquer comb and hair ornament featuring a maple leaf motif.

Shisen-do Temple

Shisen-do, now a Zen temple by the name of Jozan-ji, was originally the secluded mountain villa of Ishikawa Jozan, a retainer of the shogun Tokugawa Ieyasu. At some point it became known as Shisen-do due to the portraits of thirty-six immortal Chinese poets (*shisen*) and their poems inside. A stream runs through a garden covered in pristine white gravel. The garden features a host of flowers to delight throughout the seasons, including wisteria, irises, hydrangeas, bush clover, and sasanqua camellias.

18 永観堂 Eikan-do Temple

This two-tiered pagoda of Eikan-do offers magnificent views of Kyoto. The temple, renowned for its autumn tints since early times, was founded in 863. Originally a tantric prayer hall, it became known as Eikan-do in Heian times, when it was converted to a Jodo Shu prayer hall by the priest Eikan. A corridor traverses the maple-covered hillside, connecting the eaves of the various halls. The Amitabha image in the main hall is known as the "Turning Amida" in reference to its backward-facing visage.

19 西行堂 Saigyo-do Temple

Despite its proximity to the bustling Yasaka Shrine, the thatched-roof main building of Saigyo-do, wreathed in autumn colors, resembles an idyllic scene from deep in the hills. Legend has it this is where the famous late Heian-period poet Saigyo (1118–90) wove his grass hermit's hut, but the site lay abandoned long after his departure until reconstruction in 1893.

20 法然院 Honen-in Temple

Honen-in, marked by its thatched main gate, is said to be the site of a retreat built by Honen Shonin for Buddhist training. In 1680 it was revived as a prayer hall, and is now a temple of the Jodo Shu. Visitors can view the Amitabha principal image from in front of the austere main hall, amid the crisp mountain air. The interior of this hall is usually closed to the public, but opened on special occasions, revealing Kano-school sliding doors. A tranquil temple that seduces through every season with spring growth, autumn tints, and falling camellia flowers.

RAKUSAI
Western Area

洛西

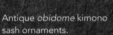

Antique *obidome* kimono
sash ornaments.

TOP: Cherry blossoms and
maple leaves

MIDDLE: Maple leaf and nutlets

BOTTOM: Gingko leaves

21 常寂光寺 Jojakko-ji Temple

One of Kyoto's most beautiful autumn sites, the view of fallen leaves sprinkled over the thatched *niomon* gate of Jojakko-ji could be taken straight from a scene in a poem. In fact, Jojakko-ji stands midway up Mt. Ogura, and was a residence of Japan's greatest medieval poet Fujiwara no Sadaie (1162–1241). Becoming a temple in the late 16th century, it quickly grew through the generosity of wealthy landowners and *daimyo* (feudal lords), eventually including a guest hall moved from Fushimi Castle as its *hondo*, and a beautiful, exquisitely proportioned two-tiered pagoda.

22 龍安寺 Ryoan-ji Temple

Originally the second home of a noble family, Ryoan-ji became a Zen temple in 1450. The *hojo* garden, surrounded on three sides by earthen walls, uses a simple composition of white gravel and fifteen rocks to represent the natural world, and has gained global renown as the epitome of the *karesansui* aesthetic. Also in the temple precincts is a pond known as Kyoyochi, the vestige of a Heian-period garden that still presents spectacular year-round floral displays. Ryoan-ji is a designated UNESCO World Heritage Site.

23 天龍寺 Tenryu-ji Temple

The shogun Ashikaga Takauji founded Tenryu-ji in 1339 to pray for the repose of the soul of Emperor Godaigo. The temple, the first of the Five Zen Mountains of Kyoto, has enjoyed great prosperity in spite of a series of fires in the feudal period. The buildings here today date from the Meiji period onward. Tenryu-ji is especially renowned for its landscape garden, which ingeniously incorporates views from faraway Arashiyama and nearby Kameyama. The temple is a designated UNESCO World Heritage Site.

24 西明寺 Saimyo-ji Temple

Saimyo-ji, a stately old temple tucked away in the hills of Makinoo, is said to have been founded in the 9th century as an annex of Jingo-ji Temple. Later destroyed during the Onin War (1476–77), it received a new lease of life in the 17th century. The principal image, a statue of Shakyamuni, is said to date from the 11th century, clear evidence of the temple's long history. A tranquil mountain temple, Saimyo-ji exudes seasonal ambience all year round, from new growth in spring to snowy winterscapes.

鹿
王
院

Rokuo-in Temple

This is the verdant bamboo approach to Rokuo-in, which began life as a sub-temple of Hoto-ji built in 1380 by the shogun Ashikaga Yoshimitsu. It subsequently fell into decay following damage during the Onin War, but its main gate and guest hall still house paintings from the brush of Yoshimitsu. The various buildings in the complex connected by corridors are interspersed with dry landscape gardens, and include a reliquary hall containing relics of the Buddha.

Traditional dry confectioneries in seasonal shapes and colors. The present style of *wagashi* (Japanese sweets) is said to have been established in Kyoto in the Edo period.

26 化野念仏寺 Adashino Nenbutsu-ji Temple

Adashino has been a burial place since the earliest times, and this temple is said to have originated with the priest Kukai (774–835), who built a small hall here and interred bones bleached by the elements. The stone Buddhas and lanterns in the grounds, numbering some 8,000, form the graves of those buried here, and every August the temple comes alive when worshippers gather for a ceremony known as the *Sento Kuyo*, in which candles are lit in memory of the dead.

27 鳥居本 平野屋 Toriimoto Hiranoya

The rustic charms of the Hiranoya Restaurant, an enduring symbol of its neighborhood for almost four centuries, ensure it remains as popular as ever. The area close to Ichi-no-torii, the approach to Atago Shrine, has remained largely unchanged for centuries, and consists of old houses nestling amongst trees forming a singular streetscape.

清凉寺

Seiryo-ji Temple

Seiryo-ji, widely known as the Shaka-do of Saga, sits on the former site of a Heian noble's villa, and was reputedly founded in 987 when a small prayer hall was built to enshrine an image of Shakyamuni. A designated National Treasure, legend has it the image came to Japan from India via China. The temple's numerous highlights include its *niomon* gate and two-tiered pagoda. Pictured here is the modern prayer hall viewed from the main hall.

29 | Otagi Nenbutsu-ji Temple

愛宕念仏寺

The late autumn sight of leaves gently falling over the 1,200 stone Buddhas in the temple precincts gives Otagi Nenbutsu-ji an ambience typical of ancient temples deep in the hills. The temple is one of Kyoto's oldest, originally constructed in Higashiyama around 770. Over the centuries Otagi Nenbutsu-ji suffered numerous setbacks—including the flooding of the Kamogawa River that swept away its buildings—but was reestablished and moved to its present location in 1922. The present *hondo* dates from the 13th century, and retains its attractive Kamakura-style visage.

30 | Enri-an Temple

厭離庵

An old temple nestled amid the serene surroundings of Sagano, Enri-an is said to be on the site of Ogura Sanso, the hillside retreat where Japan's greatest medieval poet, Fujiwara no Sadaie, compiled the *Ogura Hyakunin Isshu* anthology ("A Hundred Poems by a Hundred Poets"). Usually closed to the public, the temple is open during the changing of the colors in autumn.

61

32 神護寺 Jingo-ji Temple

Jingo-ji, situated in Takao, an area famous for its autumn scenery, was originally a small mountain temple, but in 824 it was merged with Jingo-ji in Kawachi and taken under the protection of the state as part of the government policy of *chingo kokka* (protecting and pacifying the nation through Buddhism). Later falling into disrepair, it was revived in the 12th century, and as well as boasting a fine Yakushi-nyorai (Buddha of Healing) statue with National Treasure status, the temple is home to a sizeable collection of Buddhist statues, paintings, and documents from the Heian and Kamakura periods. Of special note is the temple bell—one of the three most famous of its kind in Japan, and another National Treasure.

31 祇王寺 Gio-ji Temple

Legend has it this is where the dancing girl Gio from Japan's epic work *The Tale of the Heike* came to live as a nun. The grounds of Gio-ji are densely covered in green bamboo and maple trees, and the mossy gardens and thatched nun's retreat give the temple a special ambience. Enshrined here are wooden images of Gio, her mother Toji, and sister Ginyo, helping to bring this ancient story to life. The window in the retreat is said to cast a seven-colored shadow depending on the manner in which sunlight enters.

33 野宮神社 Nonomiya Shrine

This small shrine nestled in a bamboo forest in Sagano was originally the site where the royal princess chosen as high priestess of the Ise Jingu Shrine went into seclusion to purify herself before setting out for Ise. Nonomiya was founded around the year 800, and this black wooden *torii* gate set in spartan surroundings retains its look of antiquity. A popular destination for young women praying for good fortune in marriage.

34 宝厳院 Hogon-in Temple

A sub-temple of Tenryu-ji, built in 1461. Usually closed to the public, Hogon-in is opened every autumn. The *Shishiku* (literally "lion's roar") garden in the temple precincts is said to be of Muromachi-period vintage. This dry landscape garden, incorporating vistas of distant Arashiyama, has been famous for centuries, and frequently appeared in Edo-period garden guides. The autumn tints are exquisite, and illuminated at night.

35 金蔵寺 Konzo-ji Temple

Constructed by Imperial Decree in 718, Konzo-ji thrived throughout the Heian period as the most famous temple in the Nishiyama hills, but was later razed in successive wars. The present buildings are 17th-century reconstructions, but nestled unobtrusively deep in the hills they hint of much earlier times. North of the *hondo* are panoramic vistas from Oharano to Higashiyama, and delightful distant scenes of autumn color. The main gate, seen looking down from the top of the stairs leading up to the temple, is framed by the seasonal spactacle.

RAKUNAN
Southern Area

洛南

A *hanakanzashi* hair ornament
with a maple leaf motif

36 | Mimuroto-ji Temple

三室戸寺

Mimuroto-ji's extensive gardens are planted with some 20,000 azaleas and 10,000 hydrangea bushes that create a magnificent sight when in bloom. Founded in the mid-8th century by Emperor Konin, Mimuroto-ji was moved several times before being erected in its present location. The principal image, a gilt bronze, thousand-armed Kannon that according to legend suddenly materialized from the surrounding hills, is on public display only on the 17th day of the month.

37 石峰寺 Sekiho-ji Temple

A Zen temple said to date back to the 18th century, most of the original complex was gradually destroyed by various fires throughout its history, the only surviving areas being the guest hall and kitchens. Sekiho-ji is also the final resting place of Edo-period painter Ito Jakuchu, who is said to have spent his last years here. Lining the hill path and sitting among the bamboo behind the *hondo* is a vast collection of stone Buddhas, for which Jakuchu is said to have provided the preliminary sketches.

38 光明寺 Komyo-ji Temple

Komyo-ji, founded in 1198, is said to rest on the site where Honen Shonin first preached his doctrine of Amitabha Buddhism. Despite falling victim to a series of conflicts, including the Onin War, the complex was rapidly rebuilt, and the extensive precincts contain over thirty buildings. In autumn the stone-paved approach known as Nyoninzaka is a vision of sublime color. Komyo-ji is normally only lit up at night on special occasions.

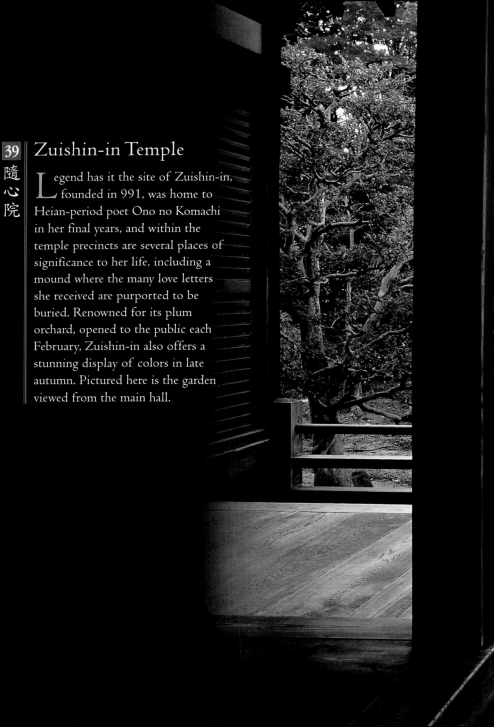

Zuishin-in Temple

Legend has it the site of Zuishin-in, founded in 991, was home to Heian-period poet Ono no Komachi in her final years, and within the temple precincts are several places of significance to her life, including a mound where the many love letters she received are purported to be buried. Renowned for its plum orchard, opened to the public each February, Zuishin-in also offers a stunning display of colors in late autumn. Pictured here is the garden viewed from the main hall.

40 城南宮 Jonangu Shrine

First built as a spiritual guardian for the south of the capital during construction of the early city of Heian-kyo in 794. Later, when retired Emperor Shirakawa built the Jonan Detached Palace, Jonangu was incorporated in it. It was used as accommodation for traveling members of the Imperial Family, and greatly revered as a place to pray for the protection of travelers. The gardens, seen here, are renowned for their exquisite seasonal displays, and attract a constant stream of visitors.

RAKUHOKU
Northern Area

洛北

Noh headbands with
Kyoto-style embroidery

蓮
華
寺

Renge-ji, nestled in the northern hills of Kyoto, was originally an old temple on Shichijo-dori abandoned after the Onin War, but given a new lease of life here in 1662. Legend has it that a number of well-known artists including Kano Tan'yu assisted with the temple's renaissance. The garden seen here from the main hall, has two islands arranged in a pond fed by a tributary of the Takanogawa River, and is a compact but particularly elegant example of Edo landscape design. A popular sightseeing spot in autumn.

42 高桐院 Koto-in Temple

Koto-in, with its delightful maple-lined approach (LEFT), was founded in 1601 as a sub-temple of Kyoto's famous Daitoku-ji temple. The *shoin* (reception hall) is said to be the former residence of the famous tea ceremony master Sen no Rikyu. The teahouse is reputed to be one that was used at a large tea ceremony hosted by the warlord Toyotomi Hideyoshi at Kitano in 1587. The *hojo* garden (ABOVE) is generally known as "The Maple Garden." While the new bloom of spring also charms, few scenes have more poetic elegance than Koto-in blanketed with fallen leaves in late autumn.

43 源光庵 Genko-an Temple

Genko-an, an austere collection of buildings on a compact site, is a Zen temple established in 1346. The *hondo*, built in 1694, includes the round "Window of Enlightenment" and square "Window of Confusion," each with its own significance in Buddhism. Beyond these windows lies a beautiful garden that bursts with vibrant color in autumn.

44 | Oharagawa River

大原川

Rising on the border between northeastern Kyoto and Shiga Prefecture, the Takanogawa River, which joins the Kamogawa River at Demachiyanagi and flows through the city, has been essential to Kyoto livelihoods for centuries, providing water for uses as diverse as agriculture and the picturesque *Kyo-yuzen* dyeing. The upper reaches of the river are known as the Oharagawa, synonymous with the atmospheric mountain village of Ohara and the crystal-clear waters of its ponds and streams.

A delicately crafted openwork round fan in the Kyoto style. The motif is influenced by traditional Japanese poetry.

45 貴船神社 Kibune Shrine

Situated in the hills of northern Kyoto, Kibune is an old shrine where the Heian-period writer Izumi Shikibu is said to have worshipped. Legend has it that a goddess once came here by boat seeking fresh water, and paid homage to the Water God. Blessed with clean, clear water and air, Kibune is a popular destination for escaping the summer heat and admiring autumn leaves.

46 宝泉院 Hosen-in Temple

Hosen-in, founded in the 12th century for the study of *shomyo* (sutra chanting employed in Buddhist rites), was the creation of the monks of the nearby Shorin-in temple. The garden viewed from the Edo-period reception hall is known literally as the "Picture-Frame Garden" and resembles a painting cut out of the temple's cool bamboo groves. Looming in the grounds is a giant 700-year-old pine tree granted natural heritage status by the city of Kyoto.

47 Iwato Ochiba Shrine

岩戸落葉神社

Iwato Ochiba Shrine is a small shrine located some twenty kilometers along the Shuzan Kaido (Route 162) in the hills to the northwest of the city. Boasting a long history, it is said to have been greatly revered by the Imperial Family in earlier times. One story has it the shrine was originally called Ochikawa Shrine, but at some point was renamed the *ochiba*, or "fallen leaf," shrine. Every year in late autumn, stately gingko trees towering over thirty meters high cover the shrine precincts in a carpet of gold.

48 | Sanzen-in Temple

三千院

The ancient *monzeki-jiin* Sanzen-in is said to have started as a small prayer hall built on Mt. Hiei in the 8th century, arriving here in Ohara in 1871 following several relocations. Buildings such as the Shinden (Dragon Hall) and guest hall stand in serene elegance in the bracing mountain air, while the Ojo-Gokuraku-in (Amitabha Hall) nestled in a cedar grove has become a potent symbol of Ohara. The Suzakumon Gate is shown at left.

Josho-ji Temple

49
常
照
寺

Maples abound in the area around the main hall of Josho-ji. The temple was built in 1616 using land donated by Hon'ami Koetsu, a founder of the Rinpa school of painting. The famous bright red Yoshino Gate, was donated by Yoshino Tayu II, the legendary entertainer and beauty of the Shimabara pleasure quarters. A lovely, atmospheric temple where spring cherry blossoms and autumn tints delight in equal measure.

An early Edo-period lacquer tea caddy. Said to be the work of legendary master craftsman Koma Ikyu (?–1683).

KYOTO AREA

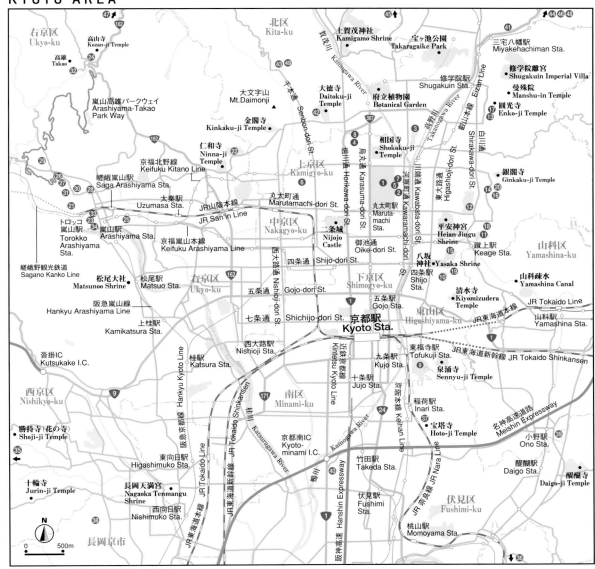

1 Kyoto Imperial Palace 京都御所
2 Rozan-ji Temple 盧山寺
3 Shimogamo Shrine 下鴨神社
4 Myoken-ji Temple 妙顕寺
5 Nashinoki Shrine 梨木神社
6 Ryuhon-ji Temple 立本寺
7 Shojoke-in Temple 清浄華院
8 Myokaku-ji Temple 妙覚寺
9 Tofuku-ji Temple 東福寺
10 Kiyomizu-dera Temple 清水寺
11 Nanzen-ji Temple 南禅寺
12 Konkaikomyo-ji Temple 金戒光明寺
13 Konpuku-ji Temple 金福寺
14 Path of Philosophy 哲学の道
15 Shoren-in Temple 青蓮院
16 Anraku-ji Temple 安楽寺
17 Shisen-do Temple 詩仙堂

18 Eikan-do Temple 永観堂
19 Saigyo-do Temple 西行堂
20 Honen-in Temple 法然院
21 Jojakko-ji Temple 常寂光寺
22 Ryoan-ji Temple 龍安寺
23 Tenryu-ji Temple 天龍寺
24 Saimyo-ji Temple 西明寺
25 Rokuo-in Temple 鹿王院
26 Adashino Nenbutsu-ji Temple 化野念仏寺
27 Toriimoto Hiranoya 鳥居本 平野屋
28 Seiryo-ji Temple 清凉寺
29 Otagi Nenbutsu-ji Temple 愛宕念仏寺
30 Enri-an Temple 厭離庵
31 Gio-ji Temple 祇王寺
32 Jingo-ji Temple 神護寺
33 Nonomiya Shrine 野宮神社
34 Hogon-in Temple 宝厳院

35 Konzo-ji Temple 金蔵寺
36 Mimuroto-ji Temple 三室戸寺
37 Sekiho-ji Temple 石峰寺
38 Komyo-ji Temple 光明寺
39 Zuishin-in Temple 隨心院
40 Jonangu Shrine 城南宮
41 Renge-ji Temple 蓮華寺
42 Koto-in Temple 高桐院
43 Genko-an Temple 源光庵
44 Oharagawa River 大原川
45 Kibune Shrine 貴船神社
46 Hosen-in Temple 宝泉院
47 Iwato Ochiba Shrine 岩戸落葉神社
48 Sanzen-in Temple 三千院
49 Josho-ji Temple 常照寺

95

RAKUCHU 洛中

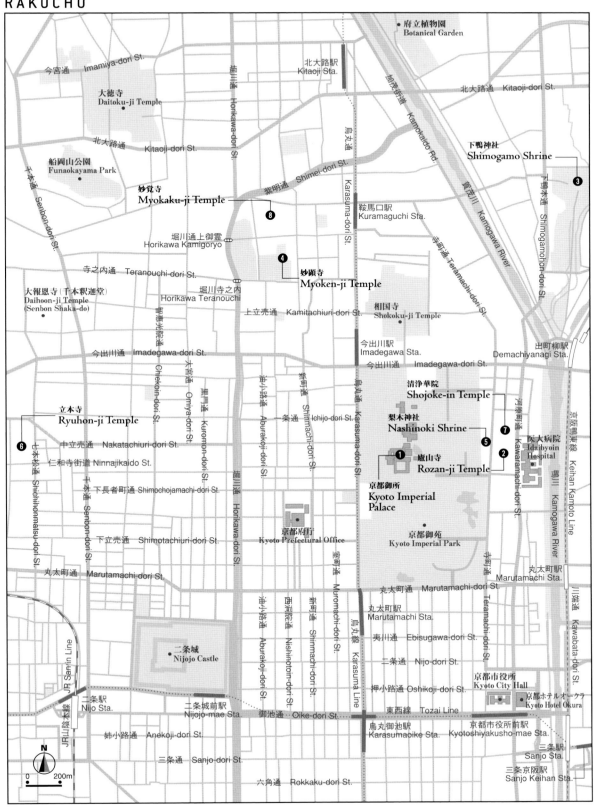

府立植物園
Botanical Garden

今宮通　Imamiya-dori St.

北大路駅
Kitaoji Sta.

大徳寺
Daitoku-ji Temple

北大路通　Kitaoji-dori St.

下鴨神社
Shimogamo Shrine
❸

船岡山公園
Funaokayama Park

北大路通　Kitaoji-dori St.

妙覚寺
Myokaku-ji Temple
❽

Shimei-dori St.

鞍馬口駅
Kuramaguchi Sta.

堀川通上御霊
Horikawa Kamigoryo

寺之内通　Teranouchi-dori St.

妙顕寺
Myoken-ji Temple
❹

大報恩寺（千本釈迦堂）
Daihoon-ji Temple
(Senbon Shaka-do)

堀川寺之内
Horikawa Teranouchi

上立売通　Kamitachiuri-dori St.

相国寺
Shokoku-ji Temple

今出川駅
Imadegawa Sta.

出町柳駅
Demachiyanagi Sta.

今出川通　Imadegawa-dori St.

今出川通　Imadegawa-dori St.

立本寺
Ryuhon-ji Temple

清浄華院
Shojoke-in Temple

梨木神社
Nashinoki Shrine
❺

❼

医大病院
Idaibyoin
Hospital

❻

中立売通　Nakatachiuri-dori St.

仁和寺街道　Ninnajikaido St.

❶ 盧山寺
Rozan-ji Temple
❷

下長者町通　Shimochojamachi-dori St.

京都御所
Kyoto Imperial
Palace

下立売通　Shimotachiuri-dori St.

京都府庁
Kyoto Prefectural Office

京都御苑
Kyoto Imperial Park

丸太町通　Marutamachi-dori St.

丸太町駅
Marutamachi Sta.

丸太町通　Marutamachi-dori St.

丸太町駅
Marutamachi Sta.

夷川通　Ebisugawa-dori St.

二条城
Nijojo Castle

二条通　Nijo-dori St.

押小路通　Oshikoji-dori St.

京都市役所
Kyoto City Hall

京都ホテルオークラ
Kyoto Hotel Okura

二条駅
Nijo Sta.

二条城前駅
Nijojo-mae Sta.

御池通　Oike-dori St.

東西線　Tozai Line

姉小路通　Anekoji-dori St.

烏丸御池駅
Karasumaoike Sta.

京都市役所前駅
Kyotoshiyakusho-mae Sta.

三条駅
Sanjo Sta.

N

三条通　Sanjo-dori St.

三条京阪駅
Sanjo Keihan Sta.

0　　200m

六角通　Rokkaku-dori St.

RAKUTO　洛東

RAKUTO

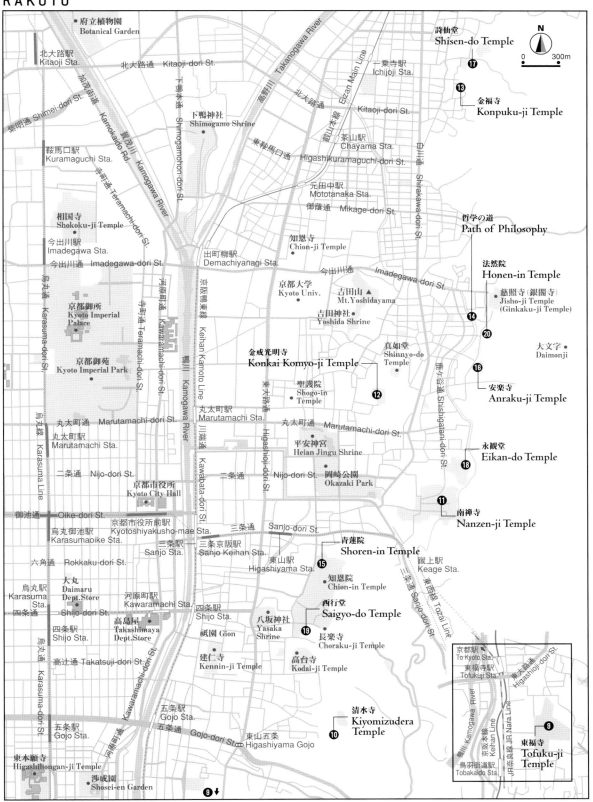

RAKUSAI 洛西

RAKUSAI

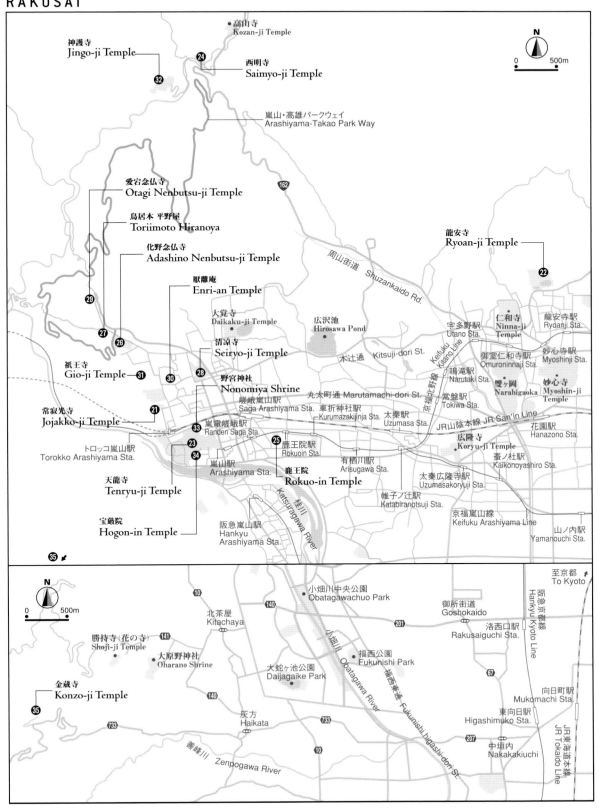

高山寺
Kozan-ji Temple

神護寺
Jingo-ji Temple

(24)

西明寺
Saimyo-ji Temple

(32)

N

0   500m

嵐山・高雄パークウェイ
Arashiyama-Takao Park Way

愛宕念仏寺
Otagi Nenbutsu-ji Temple

(162)

龍安寺
Ryoan-ji Temple

鳥居本 平野屋
Toriimoto Hiranoya

(22)

化野念仏寺
Adashino Nenbutsu-ji Temple

周山街道 Shuzankaido Rd.

厭離庵
Enri-an Temple

(29)

大覚寺
Daikaku-ji Temple

広沢池
Hirosawa Pond

宇多野駅
Utano Sta.

仁和寺
Ninna-ji
Temple

龍安寺駅
Ryoanji Sta.

(27)

(26)

清凉寺
Seiryo-ji Temple

木辻通

Kitsuji-dori St.

御室仁和寺駅
Omuroninnaji Sta.

妙心寺駅
Myoshinji Sta.

祇王寺
Gio-ji Temple

(31)

(30)

(28)

野宮神社
Nonomiya Shrine

鳴滝駅
Narutaki Sta.

雙ヶ岡
Narabigaoka

妙心寺
Myoshin-ji
Temple

常寂光寺
Jojakko-ji Temple

(21)

嵯峨嵐山駅
Saga Arashiyama Sta.

丸太町通 Marutamachi-dori St.

車折神社駅
Kurumazakijinja Sta.

常盤駅
Tokiwa Sta.

太秦駅
Uzumasa Sta.

JR山陰本線 JR San'in Line

花園駅
Hanazono Sta.

トロッコ嵐山駅
Torokko Arashiyama Sta.

(33)

嵐電嵯峨駅
Randen Saga Sta.

(23)

(34)

(25)

鹿王院駅
Rokuoin Sta.

有栖川駅
Arisugawa Sta.

太秦広隆寺駅
Uzumasakoryuji Sta.

広隆寺
Koryu-ji Temple

蚕ノ社駅
Kaikonoyashiro Sta.

天龍寺
Tenryu-ji Temple

嵐山駅
Arashiyama Sta.

鹿王院
Rokuo-in Temple

帷子ノ辻駅
Katabiranotsuji Sta.

山ノ内駅
Yamanouchi Sta.

京福嵐山線
Keifuku Arashiyama Line

宝厳院
Hogon-in Temple

桂川
Katsuragawa River

阪急嵐山駅
Hankyu
Arashiyama Sta.

(35)

N

0   500m

(10)

小畑川中央公園
Obatagawachuo Park

御所街道
Goshokaido

至京都
To Kyoto

阪急京都線
Hankyu Kyoto Line

北茶屋
Kitachaya

(140)

(201)

洛西口駅
Rakusaiguchi Sta.

勝持寺(花の寺)
Shoji-ji Temple

(141)

大原野神社
Oharano Shrine

大蛇ヶ池公園
Daijagaike Park

福西公園
Fukunishi Park

(67)

金蔵寺
Konzo-ji Temple

(140)

向日町駅
Mukomachi Sta.

(35)

灰方
Haikata

(733)

(733)

東向日駅
Higashimuko Sta.

善峰川
Zenpogawa River

(10)

中垣内
Nakakakiuchi

(207)

JR東海道本線
JR Tokaido Line

101

RAKUNAN

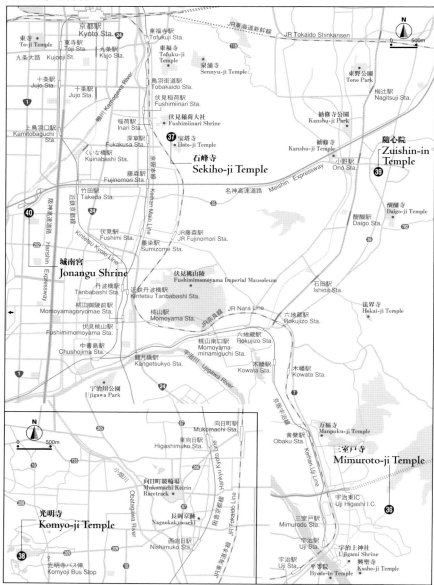

RAKUNAN 洛南

36. **Mimuroto-ji Temple** 三室戸寺
   21 Todo Shigatani, Uji-shi
   TEL: 0774-21-2067
   宇治市莵道滋賀谷21

37. **Sekiho-ji Temple** 石峰寺
   26 Fukakusa Sekihojiyama-cho,
   Fushimi-ku TEL: 075-641-0792
   京都市伏見区深草石峰寺山町26

38. **Komyo-ji Temple** 光明寺
   26-1 Ao Saijonai, Nagaokakyo-shi
   075-955-0002
   長岡京市粟生西条ノ内26-1

39. **Zuishin-in Temple** 隨心院
   35 Ono Goryo-cho, Yamashina-ku
   TEL: 075-571-0025
   京都市山科区小野御霊町35

40. **Jonangu Shrine** 城南宮
   7 Nakajima Tobarikyu-cho, Fushimi-ku
   TEL: 075-623-0846
   京都市伏見区中島鳥羽離宮町7

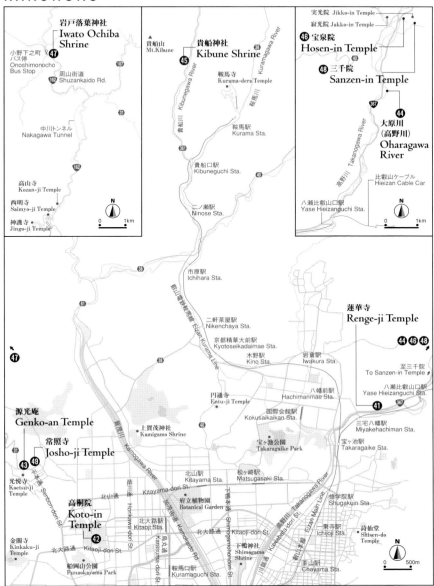

R A K U H O K U　洛北

41. **Renge-ji Temple　蓮華寺**
    1 Kamitakano Hachiman-cho, Ukyo-ku
    TEL: 075-781-3494
    京都市左京区上高野八幡町1

42. **Koto-in Temple　高桐院**
    73-1 Murasakino Daitokuji-cho, Kita-ku
    TEL: 075-492-0068
    京都市北区紫野大徳寺町73-1

43. **Genko-an Temple　源光庵**
    47 Takagamine Kita Takagamine-cho,
    Kita-ku　TEL: 075-492-1858
    京都市北区鷹峯北鷹峯町47

44. **Oharagawa River　大原川（高野川）**
    Ohara–Yase, Sakyo-ku
    京都市左京区大原〜八瀬

45. **Kibune Shrine　貴船神社**
    180 Kurama Kibune-cho, Sakyo-ku
    TEL: 075-741-2016
    京都市左京区鞍馬貴船町180

46. **Hosen-in Temple　宝泉院**
    187 Ohara Shorin'in-cho, Sakyo-ku
    TEL: 075-744-2409
    京都市左京区大原勝林院町187

47. **Iwato Ochiba Shrine　岩戸落葉神社**
    170 Ono Shimono-cho, Kita-ku
    TEL: 075-406-2877
    京都市北区小野下ノ町170

48. **Sanzen-in Temple　三千院**
    540 Ohara Raikoin-cho, Sakyo-ku
    TEL: 075-744-2531
    京都市左京区大原来迎院町540

49. **Josho-ji Temple　常照寺**
    1 Takagamine Kita Takagamine-cho,
    Kita-ku　TEL: 075-492-6775
    京都市北区鷹峯北鷹峰町1

ACKNOWLEDGMENTS

The publisher would like to thank all the following temples, shrines, companies, and organizations for graciously consenting to the use of the photographs and other material for this volume.

Adashino Nenbutsu-ji (p. 56), Aiba (p. 85: Round fan, TEL: 075-221-1460), Anraku-ji (p. 38), Chikuei-do (p. 17: *Koro* incense burner, TEL: 075-241-2636), Eikan-do (p. 42), Enri-an (p. 61), Genko-an (pp. 82–83), Gio-ji (p. 62), Hiranoya (p. 57), Hogon-in (p. 65), Honen-in (p. 44), Hosen-in (p. 87), Imperial Household Agency (pp. 10–11), Iwato Ochiba Shrine (pp. 88–89), Jingo-ji (p. 63), Jojakko-ji (pp. 46–47), Jonangu Shrine (p. 76), Josho-ji (p. 92), Kibune Shrine (p. 86), Kintake-do (p. 67: *Hanakanzashi* hair ornament, TEL: 075-561-7868), Kiyomizudera (p. 28), Komyo-ji (pp. 72–73), Konkai Komyo-ji (p. 32), Konpuku-ji (p. 33), Konzo-ji (p. 66), Koto-in (pp. 80–81), Mimuroto-ji (pp. 68–69), Miyawaki Baisen-an (p. 23: Folding fans, TEL: 075-221-0181), Myokaku-ji (p. 22), Myoken-ji (p. 16), Nakanishi Shoho-ken (p. 29: *Unkinbachi* bowl, p. 93: Lacquer *natsume* tea caddy, TEL: 075-551-8000), Nanzen-ji (pp. 2, 30–31), Nashinoki Shrine (pp. 18–19), Nonomiya Shrine (p. 64), Otagi Nenbutsu-ji (p. 60), Renge-ji (pp. 78–79), Rokuo-in (p. 54), Rozan-ji (pp. 12–13), Ryoan-ji (pp. 48–49), Ryuhon-ji (p. 20), Saigyo-do (p. 43), Saimyo-ji (pp. 52–53), Sanzen-in (pp. 90–91), Seiryo-ji (pp. 58–59), Sekiho-ji (pp. 70–71), Shimogamo Shrine (pp. 14–15), Shioyoshi-ken (p. 55: Confectioneries, TEL: 075-441-0803), Shisen-do (pp. 40–41), Shojoke-in (p. 21), Shoren-in (pp. 36–37), Tenryu-ji (pp. 50–51), Tessai-do (p. 1: Lacqer bowl, pp. 8, 45: *Obidome* kimono sash ornament, p. 39: Comb and Hair ornament, TEL: 075-531-2829), Tofuku-ji (pp. 24–27), Tokyo National Museum (p. 6: Painted screen, Image: TNM Image Archives, Source: http://TnmArchives.jp/), Toshiaki Nagakusa (Nuitsukasa Nagakusa) (p. 9: Embroidered Noh costume, pp. 77, 98, 102: Embroidered Noh headbands, pp. 96, 100: Embroidered screen, TEL: 075-451-3391), Yoshiminedera (pp. 4–5), Zuishin-in (pp. 74–75).

PHOTO CREDITS

Hidehiko Mizuno: pp. 2–3, 10–11, 14–15, 21, 24–27, 36–38, 44, 50–53, 57–59, 62, 65, 70–73, 76, 84, 86, 94

Kayu Mizuno: pp. 4–5, 28, 33, 40–43, 87

Yasutaka Ogawa: pp. 12–13, 16, 18–20, 22, 30–32, 34–35, 46–49, 54, 56, 60–61, 63–64, 66, 68–69, 74–75, 78–83, 88–92

Shuichi Yamagata (Neutral): pp. 1, 9, 17, 23, 29, 39, 45, 55, 67, 77, 85, 93, 96, 98, 100, 102

（英文版）京紅葉
Autumn Colors of Kyoto: A Seasonal Portfolio

2008年10月30日　第 1 刷発行　　　　印刷・製本所　大日本印刷株式会社

編　者　講談社インターナショナル株式会社
撮　影　水野秀比古
　　　　水野歌夕
　　　　小川康貴
発行者　富田　充
発行所　講談社インターナショナル株式会社
　　　　〒112–8652 東京都文京区音羽 1–17–14
　　　　電話　03–3944–6493（編集部）
　　　　　　　03–3944–6492（営業部・業務部）
　　　　ホームページ　www.kodansha-intl.com

落丁本・乱丁本は購入書店名を明記のうえ、講談社インターナショナル業務部宛にお送りください。送料小社負担にてお取替えします。なお、この本についてのお問い合わせは、編集部宛にお願いいたします。本書の無断複写（コピー）、転載は著作権法の例外を除き、禁じられています。

定価はカバーに表示してあります。

Printed in Japan
ISBN 978–4–7700–3093–1